TRIUMPH HOUSE
Poetry with a Purpose

CHRISTIAN CELEBRATIONS
FROM THE NORTH 2000

Edited by

Steve Twelvetree

Stella

Hughes

(PAGE 85)

First published in Great Britain in 2000 by
TRIUMPH HOUSE
Remus House,
Coltsfoot Drive,
Woodston,
Peterborough, PE2 9JX
Telephone (01733) 898102

HB ISBN 1 86161 604 X
SB ISBN 1 86161 609 O

FOREWORD

Each year Triumph House launches its regional series of poems - bringing forth to the reader a mixed blend of Christian opinions and expressions on today's modern issues. Prayers, messages of Faith and Christian perspectives on life are all shared and defined within these pages, helping the intimate bond between reader and author to be discovered. The poems may vary in both style and theme but each is a unique insight and inspiration brought to you from the power of the working mind.

This collection has been compiled from the North of the UK and celebrates the heartaches and the joys of Christian verse. In true poetic style this book is sure to both encourage and delight for many years to come.

Steve Twelvetree
Editor

CONTENTS

Not Alone	M Milliken	1
The Gutted Fish	B Pritchard	2
A Cry From Nature	M Platts	3
Goodbye	Thomas Lavelle	4
Fate	Rachel Lowdon	6
A Fleeting Glance	Albert H Gormley	7
My Daily Prayer	Mary Veronica Ciarella Murray	8
Fish On Good Friday	Margaret Cockbain	9
Baby Sitting	Dorrie McMenemy	10
Care?	I Rogerson	11
I Prayed Today	Lena Cooper	12
Some	Rita Urwin	13
The Concert	Marlene Allen	14
A New Beginning	Marjorie Lancaster	15
Shop Before You Drop	David Lord	16
Blessings	C Sill	17
Friendliness Among Christians	Marjorie Cowan	18
The Christening	June Slater	19
Out Of The Darkness	V Francis	20
Millennium Eve	John Pottinger	21
God's Voice Is Heard	Eileen Kay Bunn	22
Creator	Mazard Hunter	23
The Lord And I	Ann Brodie	24
When I Am No More	J P Walker	25
True Friendship	J Mary Kirkland	26
Journey Of Discovery (The Lost Sheep)	Tom Hicks	27
This Is My Home	Joy Francis	28
Returns To Scale	Robert D Shooter	29
You Shall Be Free	Barbara Ashworth	30
The Soloist	B Boon	32
The Millennium	Dorothy Limbert	33
The Colours Of The Four Seasons	Jean Wood	34
Redemption	Elsie Birch	35

Memories	Helen Knott	36
Praise God	Edward Christian	37
To Dream On A Whisper Of A Prayer	Hilary Anne Bannister	38
The Christmas Story	Hazel Guest	39
Yesterday	S Chrystal Wanstall	40
Peace	R Hannah	41
A Wisp Of Lace	David Wesley Cooper	42
In God's Hands	A Harrison	43
Just Believe	J Firth	44
Silent Night	Louise Swanson	45
Alice Muriel Saint	Linda Zulaica	46
In Tune With God	Olwen Counsell	47
Millennium Renewal	Leonard C Jones	48
I Am The Way, The Truth And The Life	Ann Langley	50
The Sum Of	I Squires	51
Your Love	Ian Squire	52
Destiny	Thomas H Woods	53
Who Is This?	Annie Lund	54
Our Mum	K Willmott	55
Harvest Home	Margaret Walker	56
Peace	Joan Patrickson	57
Heaven	Derek G Bond	58
I Am Here	M Guiry	59
The Mirror	B Bradley	60
Reflections	Daphne Wustrack	61
Christ's Millennium	M Oliver	62
A Position Of Trust	Brian Nichols	63
Untitled	D Finkel	64
World Peace	Michael G Salmon	65
The Way Of Salvation	Audrey Coe	66
Forget Me Not	W Lea	67
Distant Dreams	Valerie Kirwood Edwards	68
Love	Rita White	69
Outstretched Arms (Message From The Cross)	Colin Gordon-Farleigh	70
Untitled	Alex Wallace	71

If Only . . .	M Lawson	72
Communion	James E Cragg	73
A Part Of God's Creation	Joan Marsh	74
A Gift To Share	Susan Carr	75
Lord I'm Ready	Freda Ingham	76
You Must Trust In Jesus	Nick Stratford	77
Our Beloved Earth	J K Raynor	78
Rebirth	Martin Jackson	79
The Year 2000	J Earl	80
Antiseptic Communion	Alex Calveley	81
The Fall	Anne M Smithers	82
Two Thousand Years Of Jesus	Diana R Duff	84
The Five Senses	Stella Hughes	85
Listen To The Trees	Susan Mulhall	86
A Golden Memory	Yvonne O'Brien	87
Scarlet	Freda Bill	88
Mere Man	Sean Nixon-Smith	89
We Believe	J Hamilton	90
Daydreams	Margaret Turner	91
School's Out	Joan Smith	92
Unveiled	Ray Smith	94
One Puts Their Trust In God	Anne Freeman	95
Promise	Jeannine Anderson Hall	96
Father-Son	Julia Cutting	97
Do It For Me	John R Jones	98
Millennium Dream	Bessie Martin	99
Abel And Cain	Johanna Pihulak	100
The Evil That Grows	Trisha Moreton	101
Thoughts	JML	102
When You'd Like To Forget	Celia Ann Islam	103
Strolling	M Birtles	104
The Tree That Died Of Shame (The Chosen One)	G Jones	106
Freedom?	Andrew David Fisher	107
Coward	Jean Healey	108
Images Of God	T Woodhouse	109
Memories	Barbara Hampson	110
Obsservations	Alfa	111

Unity	Margaret Dolman	112
Untitled	Joseph McComas	113
Does The Dome Hide Our Sins?	Gerald M Fitzgerald	114
Child Of My Love	C Brown	115
What Is A Prayer?	Karen Husband	116
Life	Barbara Robson	117
Confidence	Kathleen Warneken	118
Life	Marshal Green	119
Morning Light	Pettr Manson-Herrod	120
Wings Of Prayer	S Binks	121
Rain	S M Hall	122
A Love So Strong	Amanda Steel	123
To A Country Lane	R Large	124
Show Me Your Word Lord	Helen Lockwood	125
Blown Roses	A A Allan	126
God's Eternal Purpose	F Sidaway	128
Jesus, My Brother	Kathleen Bishop	129
Mistrust	Marian Ball	130

NOT ALONE

My heart alone cannot defeat
All the demons in their fleet
Stood alone I would submit
To temptation's bitter grit

Every day the demons call
Put me back against the wall
All alone I'd close my eyes
And forever slowly die

But alone is not the way
With help there is a brighter day
Instead on lonely painful drain
The Lord has given me life again.

M Milliken

THE GUTTED FISH

Watching the fisherman reeling in his catch,
he smiles as,
without hesitance, removes the hook
letting the fish fall to ground.
As the air dries its rainbow scales
the fish just blankly stares,
and,
in that split second where Death takes life
the fisherman's knife ripped open its guts,
spilling them out,
but still the fish just stares.
My teardrops fall, my lost emotions held within them.
I too share that gutted feeling,
wishing my hurt could be cut out - so easily removed.
I lean over the water's edge, a second away from my
Life to death.
I call out to God for help,
then as I look down,
my eyes stare back at my own in the water's mirror.
They are not blank, nor dull, or dead,
but show a single tear that sparkles life,
life I have no right to take,
so I will leave my hurt behind,
move on,
survive.

B Pritchard

A CRY FROM NATURE

I'm Freddie Frog, I sit and croak
I'm spokesman for my friends
It really is no joke
My friends are getting scarce you see
Through man's inhumanity.

This world was not just made for man
We are all part of God's great plan
You foul the rivers, land and air but
Not content with that
You then destroy our habitat

So one by one, we will disappear
And life on earth will change.

The insects will take over and destroy
Your crops I fear.

No longer will you see a bird
Or listen to its song.
Please take notice of my friends
And try to right this wrong.

Remember God's blessing for
Creatures, great and small
Don't spoil the balance of Nature
It's important to us all

M Platts

GOODBYE

I saw her in a boat waving to me
It was so far away I could hardly see
The boat then went off into the distance
I told the lifeguard it needed some assistance.
The lifeguard then said 'What do you mean dear
No boats had been seen here since an Angel was seen on the pier.'
The boat went on into the sky
The lifeguard then followed it like he could fly
I did not know what happened that day
To be honest, nobody could say
It then came back in a dream
I'd tried to go over what I had seen
I then remember something new
Into the sea, a bottle, she threw
I went to the sea and found the bottle
I took it home and pressed on the throttle
Inside there was a note
But did it fall from the boat
So the note I read
And it said
Sorry I had to leave
But my time was up so roll up your sleeves
Please don't grieve on me
Because when the time is right I will be waiting to greet thee
But until then help our friends, our family too
And through it all you will make it through
And when new people come into your life
Tell them of me without any strife
Many years later as I found
I was up and heavenly bound
And sure enough she was there
But all I could do was sit and stare

So through our lives we will find that heartache
And pain will try to keep us behind
But if we go on we will see
That dead loved ones will be waiting to happily greet thee.

Thomas Lavelle (13)

FATE

I have often wondered what fate is
Is it something that's planned out how I will live?
Does God decide what my actions will be?
Or some other force which I can't see?

If God is this force then it's not so bad
I trust Him with my life and I'm almost glad
That He's there to guide me and help me through
Times of doubt and with making decisions too.

I trust that He'll show me the right path to take
Won't let me fall to the ground or make a mistake
He'll make sure my life is the best it can be
But what if He isn't this force I can't see?

Maybe so-called *fate* doesn't even exist
Could I be by myself? Does no one assist?
Do I have to make choices all on my own?
Is my future not made nor set down in stone?

Whatever my views on what fate be
I'm sure God will always be there to help me
If He doesn't control, then He'll guide my path
Help me reach all my goals and never turn back.

I believe my fate will be what I make
That events will proceed in the time that I take
With my level head and with God by my side
I'm sure that my future will turn out just fine.

Rachel Lowdon

A FLEETING GLANCE

I glanced across a darkened room
Our eyes they met by chance
Twinkling in those eyes I saw
More than a passing glance.

A wondrous glow flamed from her eyes
A glow to set my heart on fire
She gazed at me and she could see
I was burning with desire.

The smile she gave lit up the room
As with a fleeting, darting glance
She stole my heart, my body, my soul
Could this be my first romance?

Her lips were like the dew at dawn
Kissed by the moonbeams' waning light
The message from her innocent eyes
Filled my heart with a pure delight.

Her hair was like a field of gold
Caressed by dawn lights gentle gleams
Her eyes so blue, pierced me through
Now, this could be the girl of my dreams.

Then I spied a band upon her hand
A plain gold ring, that is true
'Twas then I knew she was not for me
And so; I began my search anew!

Albert H Gormley

MY DAILY PRAYER

Sweet Jesus look down on me
Guide me day by day
If I should waver, in thought or deed
Forgive my faults I pray.

Lead me onto the path of right
Grant me time to understand
If I should falter along the way
Turn from the route you planned
Trust me Lord to learn your ways
As time recedes
My life is in your hands.

Mary Veronica Ciarella Murray

FISH ON GOOD FRIDAY

We have fish on Good Friday, it wouldn't be right
To have meat on our plates for supper that night.

It's something to do with religion and that
Like going to church without wearing a hat.

Go to church on Good Friday, are they open that day?
I might go on Sunday if we're not going away.

I'd go every Sunday, except for the fact
That I'm working all week and by the weekend I'm *whacked.*

Mind, I play Christian tapes and I watch Songs of Praise
It saves worrying about church in these busy days.

They say standards are falling but I try to please God,
We'll have fish on Good Friday - I think I'll get cod.

Margaret Cockbain

BABY SITTING

Minding Scott for the day
I just had to pray
Please let him be good
As little boys should.

While I was praying
He looked up at me
With the cutest of smiles
That I ever did see.

I knew God was listening
He put the smiles there
What better way to answer my prayer?

He soon fell asleep
And low and behold
He awoke with a smile
A joy to behold.

Minding Scott for the day
Was really a pleasure,
God's gift from above
I give thanks in full measure.

Dorrie McMenemy

CARE?

Nobody child, nobody mother
Bony frame
Has no name
Does anybody care for the nobody child
In a barren land where life is cheap?
Poverty stricken, living off a rubbish heap
There are nobody children living like rats down a sewer.
Kill them says somebody so there will be fewer
Anyway says somebody who cares
I say - God cares - so somebody beware.

I Rogerson

I Prayed Today

Lord, freeze my heart if it must feel again
The hurt of loss - the agony of pain.
For all the time, there was - or so it seems,
No end to its high hopes - romantic dreams.
It gave out then a joyous rhythmic beat
When love was everything and life complete.

No more - no more - no more - it is all done.

Wait - please wait, this heart wants to be alive
To prove it has the courage to survive,
Face another loss - bear the extra pain.
It yearns to come to life, to live again.
A frozen heart will need a lot of sun,
Your blessing too, Lord - when the day is done.

Lena Cooper

SOME

Dear Lord I pray to thee
Hear my friends as they call upon thee
Some are in sorrow, some in pain
Some in joy as they praise your name.

Whatever prayer they send to you
I know Lord you will see them through.

Some are young, some are old
Some believe, some don't
Whatever prayer they send to you
I know your love will reach them too.

Some will listen and obey
Some will shrug and turn away
But you dear Lord will always be
Their friend and saviour for Eternity.

Rita Urwin

THE CONCERT

The Parish arranged a concert
To honour St Mary at Hesket,
For it was the Patronal Festival;
The church wore its best *bib and weskit.*

The place was filled to the gunnels,
No room e'en for a church mouse.
The vicar bade us all welcome,
And the lights went down on the house.

There were splendid solo performances
On the organ, guitar and violin,
And some *Cummerlan Teals* to delight us,
With a bit of the blarney thrown in.

The Brownies sang, the school choir sang
And the church choir played its part too;
There were karaoke and dancing
And tap to the St Louis Blues.

The finale was the *Last Night of the Proms*
With everyone present singing.
I doubt if Hesket's ever heard the like;
It sets the rafters ringing!

I hope that St Mary enjoyed the show
As she watched us, perhaps from the wings.
I think she did, for I myself
That night heard the angels sing.

Marlene Allen

A New Beginning

Night dark - of stars no spark,
No moon - it's clouded o'er;
Curtains pulled tight to keep out the night,
Shut fast is every door.
Wind cold - sheep in fold,
Shepherds are dozing awhile
Breathing slow. What do they know
Of the imminent birth of a child?
One star afire - heavenly choir,
Kings, wise men and shepherds, too,
Kneel at the feet of the infant so sweet,
As they worship the Saviour that's new.

Marjorie Lancaster

SHOP BEFORE YOU DROP

The greatest purchase of them all
Will not be bought in your fancy shopping mall
In a deserted supermarket at ten past one
Down the aisle with the two for one
In the back of a car on a Sunday morning
On a scruffy car park as the day is dawning
Down the back street in the discount store
With electrical goods wanted no more
In the High Street stores of famous names
With designer labels and overpriced games.

This greatest purchase comes for free
No salesman's commissions and no set up fee
You won't spend your money and then wonder why
It's not gaudily advertised to get you to buy
No credit allowed and no interest free
There are no fancy loans and no expletive HP
Cash is not taken and plastic not asked for
There's no tiny print straining your eyes more
No increased cost for a lifetime guarantee
Best of all this gift comes for free.

The gift from God, a gift for all
Can be found everywhere, not just in a church hall
We all have a chance if we want to receive
All that he asks is we choose to believe
The contract is out and ready to sign
Open your heart that's the first sign
The sale is your life with rules we can't bend
One day this sale must come to an end
The chance to receive will one day come to a stop
It's simply a case of shop before you drop.

David Lord

BLESSINGS

Thank God for the harvest, the plentiful store.
Rejoice for the crops brought in safely once more.
The storms of winter - they may do their worst
So gather crops early and get in there first.
Thank now your Father for all that is good
And give Him the praise in the way that you should.
Join fellow Christians in church on this day
And give Him the thanks in the usual way.
Always be grateful for joys shown to you
But do not forget those who've need of them too.

C Sill

FRIENDLINESS AMONG CHRISTIANS

They're a friendly gathering at a coffee morning and Bring and Buy
And to attend them all you really should try
At other people's churches besides the one you attend,
And discussing general topics, you can sometimes make a friend.

Most stalls have books and cosmetics too,
Discuss the books you like and the make up that suits you
Discuss coming socials at your church's venue,
And maybe they'll come along to some with you.
All church-goers should gather together much more,
They're all aiming for the same thing, to reach Heaven's door.

Marjorie Cowan

THE CHRISTENING

Into the world
with first breath of air
Chloé came for you to care.

Your love together
now strengthened even more
when two became three
opening up a new door.

So you pass through
to a world of love
from those around
and God above.

Your daughter in whose thanks we give
the promise of His faith to love.

June Slater

OUT OF THE DARKNESS

Glory be, can this be me
Living life so peacefully?
Stress and strife affect me not,
Anger, temper, not a jot!

In case the reader now supposes
My life has been a bed of roses,
I must be clear, I get my share
Of crosses that I have to bear.

My inner light is shining bright,
It shines by day and shines by night.
It's shining when my life's a mess,
In times of trial and distress.

Great Spirit, thank you for the light
That keeps me always in your sight.
With each immortal soul I'll share
And try to shine it everywhere.

You gave me opportunity
For my advancement, spiritually.
Appreciating this, I strive
To help all those on earth to thrive.

To do some good for all mankind,
For those whose spirit eyes are blind,
Is my life's mission. With Spirit's aid
Great differences can be made.

V Francis

MILLENNIUM EVE

The vigil of millennium eve
brings flooding in
the shadows of all long lost days,
while nostalgic tears draw on
the coming times;
starting for one
what for another ends.

However many thousand years
since Jesus' birth
the openness of love
knows neither
dawn nor setting sun.

Be life a day, a month,
a million years;
I only know
no date can break
His beautiful and
everlasting reign.

John Pottinger

GOD'S VOICE IS HEARD

I sense God's voice inside me; then turn to Him and pray,
'O Lord, please help me understand just what You want to say.
You tell me that You love me; You tell me that You care:
I know You want to help me - so why, Lord, can't I hear?'

I cannot hear the songbirds or pitter-patter rain.
But when I ask, 'Why me Lord?' You carefully explain . . .
'You see, I love you dearly; I want you close by me.
You are so very special; it's how it's meant to be.

The hearing I gave voices to *talk* the Truth from God,
But look! I gave you hands to sign, in beauty, without words.
Oh yes, you're very special because you cannot hear;
I hold you close beside me - you've nothing else to fear.

The hearing have to listen to understand my Word,
Responding - but distracted to what they have just heard.
I want my special children to know just what I say
Without distracting noises when I call them to pray.

So do not feel despondent, rejected or unloved:
I hold you close, next to my heart, like hands within a glove.
You know I'm talking to you; my message loud and clear -
I love you very dearly. That's why you're deaf, my dear!'

Eileen Kay Bunn

CREATOR

How can I prove you're the Creator?
How can I prove what I feel?
Some say you're a figment of man's imagination,
But I know you're are magnificently real.
Some say this world we live on
Just happened, and in it you had no hand,
But I know every atom of creation
Was marvellously wonderfully planned.

How can I help them believe Lord?
How can I help them see?
That you are the maker of
Sky, land and sea.
How can I help them know Lord
The one who fashioned it all.
Prairie, jungle, desert ocean and mountain tall.

I will place them in your hands, Lord,
Pray that like me they will heed your call,
Then they will know you're the Creator
God and Father, Lord over all.

Mazard Hunter

THE LORD AND I

The joy I feel in God's loving care,
I'd like to spread around and share.
I can't believe I feel so good,
I never really thought I would.
It took so long to find you Lord,
I'd never listened to your word.
But now at last I know what's right
I pray to you almost every night.
I try to live a life that's good,
Helping others like I know I should.
So when you're feeling down and sad,
Pray to the Lord, and you'll be glad.
For when you feel His presence there
You'll know He's listened to your prayer
So spread the word from friend to friend
You'll find true happiness in the end.
I did!

Ann Brodie

When I Am No More

When I am no more, when I am gone from you
Think of me not in tears but remember the good.
Times we had through the years.

Look around you as you go on your way, see me in
A flower, smell its perfume and I am there.

Listen in the silence you will hear me call, I'm
The song of a bird on your garden wall
Soak up the sunshine and laugh in the rain
Memories that come to you will take away the pain.

When I am no more remember this life is what
You make of it. Don't sit and sigh, lift up
Your head and don't let life pass you by.
Try to be brave
And think of yesterdays with a smile.

J P Walker

TRUE FRIENDSHIP

True friendship lasts forever
True friendship never ends
True friendship is unending
For years and years on end.
Sometimes a thread is broken
And leaves a great big hole
It's difficult to mend it
Once more to make it whole.
It brings a lot of sadness
Despair, lost hope and tears
An empty gap of nothing
Lost hope, lost love and fears.
But threads they can be mended
They can be joined again
With love and understanding
With silence, smiles and pain.
So how about an olive branch
With stitches of all kinds
To mend a hole of emptiness
To mend a breach of time.

J Mary Kirkland

JOURNEY OF DISCOVERY (THE LOST SHEEP)

Oh were I but a child again
To view life through unclouded eyes,
Excitement thrilling through each vein
And wonder stretched beyond the skies,
On tiptoe I would peep at Heaven
At four or five or six or seven.

Then would my love be unconfined
And unconditional my trust,
To all impurities be blind
Impervious to dirt and dust.
I'd live within a sparkling state
At five or six or seven or eight.

Should I feel anger now and then
Demand my will or stamp my feet,
I'd quickly learn to count to ten,
Recapture paradise complete.
And still my glorious world would shine
At six or seven or eight or nine.

If papers, radio, TV,
Should try to rob me of my prize,
Draw out the faults that lie in me,
Obscure the line twixt truth and lies
I'd strive to find my world again
At seven or eight or nine or ten.

Through all the years that would remain,
Through doubts and insecurity,
Through all my struggles to regain
That love and truth and purity
I'd learn that Heaven must stoop to me
To touch my soul and set me free.

Tom Hicks

THIS IS MY HOME

I sat awhile and watched the sea
With seagull songs surrounding me
Amidst the blue and freshest air
The scent of summer everywhere.

The waves rolled calmly over sand
A pier, in view, like outstretched hand
Brought thoughts to me of what life brings
Of feelings, cares and love and things.

And then my heart poured strength anew
As showers of hope came shining through
For on this seashore God was there
His love cascaded everywhere.

I looked towards a tower so high
That touched the vastness of the sky
And felt a sense of wondrous ease
Now captured in the soft cool breeze.

I ran my fingers through the sand
Each tiny grain fell from my hand
Reminding me of nature's way
Which God provides from day to day.

Then all my heart was blessed with pride
And with the seagull songs did glide
In sun and sand, in fresh and cool
This is my home - this is Blackpool.

Joy Francis

RETURNS TO SCALE

The woman at the well, drinks for us all,
linking thirsts, from first and second Adam,
long draughts from living water radical

swallowing through the centuries total
communion, salvation, an item
the woman at the well drinks for us all.

Post capitalism's sabbatical
for re-invention of the wheel; a dam,
long draughts from living water radical,

communism and benevolence call
realises at base, spirit does cram,
the woman at the well drinks for us all

Atheist, Jew, Christian, comparable
at needing such a basic single dram, -
long draughts from living water radical

only Kosovo, nail bomb graphical
defeat alternative shows present sham.
The woman at the well drinks for us all
long draughts from living water radical.

Robert D Shooter

YOU SHALL BE FREE

You were born in sin, there's no escape,
no way for you to be.
A perfect human being, always you will see,
your nature rising up to spoil, the
good that you would do.
Your efforts will be futile, your
triumphs will be few.
For mankind had to touch the tree,
his self-will to assert,
and his reward, ability to taint
and spoil and hurt.
Then trapped within his knowledge
the evil nature gained
a foothold on the human race,
and could not be contained.

The Great Creator looking down,
from His Almighty throne,
Had pity on our plight and
came to save us for His own.
Who else could set the record
straight and cancel out the sin,
For now, there was not one, without
a thought of self within.
And so He came, from glory torn,
to dwell in this dark place,
And all the evils of this world, He
was prepared to face.
They raged themselves against Him,
and in His darkest hour
He held His ground, victorious,
and tipped the scales of power.

The enemy defeated, stripped of
meaning here below
The love of God had conquered
without a single blow.
So Praise the name of Jesus,
He meets your every need
For if the Son shall make you free
You shall be free, indeed.

Barbara Ashworth

THE SOLOIST

He sang alone from dawn to dusk
There were no other birds,
They left him there to sing his song
Hidden in the blossom of a lilac tree.
And as I worked with rake and spade,
The evening sunset almost gone,
Still the thrush kept singing a lovely melodious song.
I really felt so flattered
That he for me should sing
When all the sky was there for him
To spread his tiny wings.
As darkness fell the birdsong stopped
As if upon a stage a curtain had been dropped,
The show was over, a silence fell.
As I rise to go two soft notes he sang
Like the sound of a last Amen.

B Boon

THE MILLENNIUM

As the millennium year approaches,
Man's achievements seem to be -
The things which occupy most minds
To keep for posterity.

But the real reason we should celebrate
Is often forgotten by this world.
Since Jesus came upon this scene,
Two thousand years've unfurled!

He came to show us peace and love,
And teach us to behave;
And yet He was rejected
By those He came to save!

He led a perfect, humble life,
And spoke such precious things.
He is, indeed, our dearest friend,
Yet He is King of Kings!

He's still alive and offers us
Salvation - full and free.
He died, and rose, that we might live
With Him eternally!

Now - if only we acknowledge
God's our Creator Lord,
And His 'Maker's instructions'
Are contained within His word.

Then the Dome would be significant;
The Truth it should convey -
Your Christian heritage honoured
In a most appropriate way!

Dorothy Limbert

THE COLOURS OF THE FOUR SEASONS

White land locked seagulls are silhouetted
Battling against dark grey snow clouds.
They circle a space of blue like a sailor's patch.
Then in a breath, a multi coloured rainbow
Spans the dull vale of stripped black branches.
A robin hops into view to complete the winter scene.

Through all shades of yellow the daffodils nod
To pink blossom trees. Slate grey pigeons menace
The brown ploughing, transformed now by emerald shoots
The hedges, green as though by a painter's hand
Shelter the wash - white lambs in gambolling mood.
God's miracle spring has returned.

Joy abounds as blue swallows dip to feed
On bordered colours as many as Joseph's coat.
Scarlet roses on the old stone wall
Mingle with vetch, where bees and butterflies toil.
Deep lilac, cream cowslips, elder and lime
Scent the summer days - a palette of hues.

The last pink foxglove falls near the purple heath.
Grey squirrels gather the sun browned nuts.
Gold is the harvest and brown are the leaves.
Ripened orchards and hedgerows berries so bright
Now the mists dim the countryside shades
The year circles to autumn as colour now fades.

Jean Wood

REDEMPTION

Not this man, the man from God,
Who healed the sick, raised the dead,
To the multitude gave bread,
Caused lame to walk, blind to see,
Captives bound by sin set free.

Not this man, the man from God,
Hanging there between two thieves,
Sounds of jeers. His mother grieves.
Why the cross, the pain, the shame,
When in Him was found no blame.

Yes this man, the man from God,
Pascal lamb sins sacrifice,
Sinless, for sin paid the price,
Entering the Holy place,
His blood redeemed fallen race.

Yes this man, the man from God,
His borrowed tomb firmly sealed.
But powerful death had to yield.
He arose! He led the way,
Sin and death no more a prey.

See this man, the man from God,
Exalted, the Holy One.
Redeemer, God's precious Son.
By His grace we share a part,
His life in us fills our heart.

See this man, the man from God,
Jesus, Saviour, faithful friend,
Promised us His spirit send,
To show us truths, be our guide,
A comforter to abide.

Elsie Birch

MEMORIES

Gone are the days when we saw firelight
Flickering on the wall
When we sat in silence
Listening to the embers fall.
We saw pictures in the fire
When the coal was all aglow
Then we spoke of memories
Of long, long ago.
No television to distract you
As we sat there roasting our knees
Watching the slices of toast did not burn
For they were the main course for tea.
Such simple pleasures we enjoyed
As we lived from day to day
Friends and neighbours were there when you needed them
And there was nothing to pay.
Just a sincere thank you
And the offer of a nice cup of tea
The gratitude that you felt for them
Was there for all to see.

Helen Knott

PRAISE GOD

Praise God in His earthly temple,
Praise Him in His heavenly temple,
Praise Him for His mighty deeds,
Praise Him for His perfect goodness.
(Psalm 150:1-2)

Praise God in the temple
With a full heart sing His praise.
Praise God on the hilltop.
To His Heaven, raise your gaze.
Praise God on the seashore
For all His mighty deeds.
Praise God on the highway:
How perfectly He leads.

Praise God down the high street.
So too, praise Him in your home.
Praise God where'er you meet
And along each path you roam.
Praise God in the green field
For all His lovely seeds,
And for every life healed:
How perfectly He leads.

Edward Christian

To Dream On A Whisper Of A Prayer

Whisper a prayer encompass it with dreams
As angels gently appear on clouds of beams
Those beautiful harmonies of light
Captured as a flicker of translucent delight
Essences of love so sweetly sung
A tasteful wonder of things to come
The conscious mind passes through
The thoughts of a revitalising energy force
All dreams are kindred spirits attaching
Themselves to sparks of life
As the dreams cascade like shimmering stars
Reflecting rainbows as they materialise
The resting prayer sleeps on the tips of every whisper
Only to be awakened by that artisan of wonder.

Hilary Anne Bannister

THE CHRISTMAS STORY

Once again it is Christmas time
A time of happiness and joy
Smiling faces round the tree
As children opened parcels with glee.

Mum and Dad watch the delightful scene
With loving smiles and eyes aglow
As their loved ones searched
For presents they knew, Santa left below.

It is a time for children who, too gave with joy
The hanky Kate had made for Mother,
Carefully wrapped, placed on the tree with the other,
The keyring Mark had made for Father.

Mother had proceeded to lay the table
With food she had lovingly prepared,
The Christmas crackers on each side plate
All these things said someone cared.

As each face glowed with love and joy
Spare a thought for the baby boy
Who was born to a virgin, in a stable
We thank God, for the little child Jesus.

Who became our Saviour and taught us
How to love one another, to be grateful, to
God for his precious gift from above
Who became our beloved Lord, our God of love.

Hazel Guest

YESTERDAY
(Dedicated to Sharleen)

Yesterday I was alone,
Afraid of what was meant to be,
Unable to face the truth,
That others could see.

Today I am full of sorrow,
Unsure how to feel,
When I finally awoke,
To confront the truth,
That was within.

Tomorrow, I will cry,
For the person I was,
Who was unable to face the truth,
That others could see.

And when I cry,
I will cry,
Releasing the anguish,
Embracing the truth,
To feel the absolution,
That was waiting for me.

S Chrystal Wanstall

PEACE

It's quiet now.
I stand on the shore
To the far horizon
The sea is calm.

Behind me, torment.
My shoulders bear the burden.
Would that I could
Stroll across the waters,
Leaving all behind.
My spirit calm,
My troubles gone.

But no.
It's not for me
To walk upon the sea.

As I gaze,
The rippling waves
Go silent.
What is that I see?

An arm raised pointing
To me.
A voice gently speaks
'Forgive, forget.'

I turn to where he's pointing,
All is calm.
I turn again
To say my thanks.
He's gone,
His job is done,
Peace of mind has returned.
Thank you.

R Hannah

A WISP OF LACE

I hide away my true intentions
My true self is held prisoner
In violent evil dimensions
Truth is never found
By my own chains I am bound
Lying saying, I am strong
Telling lies, I am also wrong
Clothes protect a skin so bad
Smiles protect a face so sad
My money grows
And my sorrow flows
I want happiness
No matter what form it takes
I want happiness until it breaks
So I live a happiness that fakes
If I'm true I hate my race
Humans are sick, perverse, a disgrace
My life is a wisp of lace
Lace stained, ripped, with a disfigured face
Judged on beauty or ugly is my race
Words and music invade my mind
It doesn't always make me kind
Jealousy eats away
The man that I am today
I don't want this to be so
Please let me go
Lay down and follow
It is a bitter pill to swallow . . .

David Wesley Cooper

IN GOD'S HANDS

I met a young girl walking down the street
Her face showed signs of pain
How could I help, what could I do
To ease away her pain?

Mummy has told me we are alone for now
Daddy has gone to fight
He went off with a band to a distant land
His buttons shining bright.

Mummy and I kissed him goodbye
We all hugged each other
As he walked away, I heard him say
Would mummy share our love with his mother.

I told her I had been like her daddy, many years ago
He would think of them, all of the time, as he battled
With the foe
His love for her would never die and to never be afraid
The Lord above would protect her daddy, a love
That's Heaven made.

A Harrison

JUST BELIEVE

Niggling thoughts, anxieties and tensions,
These needless pressures hold onto me.
Be still my heart when worrying thoughts
Disturb my peace, relax and allow
This burden to depart.
My reflection shows downward lines and frowns,
Suddenly, opening clouds reveal
Lightness and warmth, dark clouds disappear.
I feel elated, my step lightens.
Pressure is removed.
I count my blessings for they are many,
So let us listen to that inner voice,
And follow the teachings given to man.

J Firth

SILENT NIGHT

Silent night,
Holy night.
A night so dark that blackness
Haunted each corner, and stars
Buried in the Heavens, reflections.
Of we people, who knew this night was ours.
Three men, grey and lined and dusty eyed,
Saw a sign, a blazing, burning light.
They followed until it came and stayed
Over a barn and broke the night.
And the people came, knelt and prayed,
For there inside, in softest pastel light,
Lay a woman, dark as winter's wood.
Blades of straw streaked in her hair
And the air she breathed was blood.
A cry, a pained and saddened cry
Pierced the eerie stillness, and there,
Held in her arms, a small brown soul,
Deep dark-eyed and bare.
Yet this Madonna raised her head,
And spoke upon her small child's cry,
'I call him Jesus, my Son of God,'
And a tear slid from her shining eye.

Louise Swanson

ALICE MURIEL SAINT

We have our share of troubles, Mam.
Yet straight we always stand
Knowing that our faith in prayer
Will always lend a hand.
We recognise each other's pain
And both believe in hope,
Trusting that this bond we have
Will help each other cope.
Laughing, crying, living life,
Struggling with our grief.
Accepting that our time on earth
Is all so very brief.
Since Pop did join the angels high
Three years ago today
We know and understand deep down
He's just a breath away.
So come the time when, when souls unite
The angels they will say . . .
'Muriel Saint . . . We told you Bill
Was just a hug away.'

Linda Zulaica

In Tune With God

God alone makes the
Sun to shine
God alone makes
It rain
Millenniums come and
Millenniums go
But these things
Remain the same
Do you look for
A magic wand
To wave
To make
All bright and new
I'm sorry my friend
But in the end
What happens
Is up to you.

Olwen Counsell

MILLENNIUM RENEWAL
(Helped By Jesus' Bethlehem Mother)

May my love, dearest Mary,
For Jesus, never vary,
Sweet as First Communion
Constant through re-union;
Pray to the mighty lover
To help me rediscover
The reward of Mary-ways
All sweet communion days.

To love Him more, my heart still prays
For inspired joys of Christ-filled days,
Begging favours with thankful praise,
Knowing full well renewal pays
Worthwhile rewards, in countless ways;
Brightening hours with sunshine rays,
Thus giving me through each dark phase,
Increasing hope, thereby much raised.

Begone temptation's sinful charm,
Which does my mind eternal harm
When loving God - I love you so!
And Mary too - thus ever know!
Thanks to God, so very rarely
Help fails when asked by Mary
Throughout the millennium maze,
To ensure Christ-filled *Mary-days*!

Yes! Thanks to God, very rarely
Help fails through kind Mother Mary;
Her, too, all times, I'll give true love,
To please my Saviour up above;
And strive to do God's holy will,
Although at times when all uphill
Ever concerned with Mary's ways
To ensure Christ-filled *Mary-days!*

Leonard C Jones

I AM THE WAY, THE TRUTH AND THE LIFE
(John 14:6)

He left his home in Heaven
To tread upon this earth
To bring light into the darkness
And bring about new birth.

He came to conquer death and sin
And from bondage set us free
To tell us of his father's love
He died for you and me.

Now to the father we can come
Without guilt or condemnation
For Jesus died upon the cross
That we may know salvation.

Ann Langley

THE SUM OF

One, two, three, four,
Carry on to reach a score;
Call them years, multiply by five,
At one century you'll arrive;
Times this hundred years by ten,
The first millennium you've reached then;
Double this, you've travelled far,
The second millennium, here we are;
Remember - two thousand years ago?
God's Son was sent from Heaven you know!
He led us then to show the way,
His Spirit can lead us still, today;
What does all this add up too.
Thoughts, about what we will do?
Our first steps on the road to *three,*
There, by His grace our Lord will be;
The tides God made will ebb and flow,
The sun will radiate its glow;
Night will always turn to day,
God will hear us when we pray;
Miracles, can still occur,
Engineered by - Three In One - up there;
In a Dome, or wherever you might be,
Keep open eyes and mind, to see;
The truth the way the light of life,
Know the power, that overcomes all strife,
A thought, a word, your message is heard,
By God, the Creator of all, from the word;
So step out upon the miles ahead
Remembering, who is still with us, and the way He led.

I Squires

YOUR LOVE

Your love cuts my veins apart
Your love pierces the empty heart,
Your love knows all pain to bear
Your love knows the grief we share,
Your love goes on and on
Your love keeps no score of wrong,
Your love calls me by my name
Your love takes away my blame,
Your love holds me in your gaze
Your love sets my life ablaze,
I give you all my heart,
I give you all my soul,
My Lord and Saviour,
Make me whole.

Ian Squire

DESTINY

Beneath blue sky wild waves beat on the shore,
March winds blow free, tall trees all heavenward climb,
Above my head a panoply unfolds,
And all of God's creation is displayed.

Across my vision, birds and insects fly,
Beneath my feet blind worms in darkness glide,
I breathe the air, and skip with childlike glee,
Not knowing what the future may betide.

Too soon youth's short sweet span is dead and gone,
Time will not heed alas my ageing gait,
Steadfastly t'wards life's end I staunchly move,
Apace my sprightly destiny draws on.

The womb my start, my end will be the tomb,
Unless God in His wisdom, gives me grace.
It's only then my life may be explained,
When listening to the Master face to face.

With such a future why cling on, I ask,
To life with all its suffering and pain?
Only one reason can support my ploy,
For it's my human nature to remain.

Essentially, all parts of what I am,
While dwelling here in ignorance below,
And though in God's own image I was cast,
His system's based on . . . what I need to know.

Thomas H Woods

WHO IS THIS?

Blood shot eyes and thorn torn brow,
Blood dripping o'er his face,
Blood gushes from his sword thrust side:
Who is this in disgrace?

The sky is black, the thunder roars,
Flashing lightening floodlights him,
Men and soldiers shrink in fear;
Women's eyes are wet and dim.

Men shake the dice; God shakes the earth,
The man thirsts and gasps for breath:
Some hope to see a miracle;
What they see - is death.

Jews are thrilled; Romans relieved;
His followers puzzled and sad,
Then, three days on - the stone is gone,
He's alive! Rejoice! Be glad.

This power-filled person's eyes reveal
More light than suns can bring;
His presence permeates the air;
He's Christ, Redeemer; Lord and King.

Annie Lund

OUR MUM

She was only small, gentle and kind
More love and devotion you'd never find,
It is greater to give than to receive,
If you'd known our mum, these words you'd believe.

We said before she was gentle, but strong
As Samson when his hair was long,
Compassion and love for everyone,
This was the life of our dear mum.

United with Dad, the love of her life
They were an example of man and wife,
Together through all that life could give,
We'll never forget them as long as we live.

To follow this example is our intent
As hard as obeying the ten commandments,
If all thro' the world we're just like these
I'm sure we'd have a world of peace.

K Willmott

HARVEST HOME

Among the fields of golden corn
along the fabric of the jade and amber hills
the cloak of autumn spreads and sheds the rust
red leaves upon the ground.
As we worship Him in wonder of the skills
that still astound us and abound,
for we believe and trust His wisdom
as the seasons ebb and flow,
winter, spring and summer blessings,
now the harvest time we know.
Mystical in ancient legend
melancholy time of year, giving us the joy
or worship for the bounties that appear.
Glory to His awesome presence,
sanctify our harvest fare.
Be our ever faithful Father
and our autumn bounties share.

Margaret Walker

PEACE

Then comes the night, it seems from some far galaxy.
Peace and quietness, the stillness of the night.
God's answer, to the day, rest body, soul and mind
To give us strength anew, for yet another day.
And at the dawn, comes forth that other day
To weary us with pain, and endless grief anew
Then at the end of my life's day
Let there be peaceful night
And all the dreams of Heaven be true
In that eternal night.

Joan Patrickson

HEAVEN

How do you see Heaven?
Does everyone wear robes of white?
Do they have summer and winter?
Is there both day and night?

Does everyone join the choir?
Or just those who sing well,
Only one ever came back,
But about this he didn't tell.

Do we all sit or stand in sects?
Roman Catholic next to C of E,
Quakers right, Methodists the left.
And what about the likes of me?

Who is not going to be there?
Who is going to be left out?
The ones who say nothing,
Or those who sing and shout.

Who else will go to Heaven,
The Muslim and the Jew,
Is there room for the Bahi
The Buddhist and the Hindu.

I don't know if I'll make it,
And I don't know about you,
I know Jesus will be there,
And this is very true.

Derek G Bond

I AM HERE

Son I am the one who gives you strength
In the days of tribulation
Let me be your comfort now
For I will be with you in your jubilation.

Is it temptation that worries you?
Stand firm and persevere,
For when you think you are all alone
That is the time I am very near.

Let not your heart be troubled
Neither let it be afraid,
Think not yourself forsaken
For a ransom for you I paid.

So when you are afflicted
Resign yourself to my will
Let not your heart be troubled now
For I am with you still.

M Guiry

THE MIRROR

I look in the mirror and what do I see?
Whose is the face staring back at me?
It cannot be mine. I'm young I'm not old.
And still quite a charmer or so I've been told!
But there are some wrinkles; at least one or two.
And grey hairs? Reluctantly more than a few.
So where has she gone to, the girl I once was?
I don't understand it. Not really, because
I feel like a youngster, a nippy bright thing.
But seeing's believing. When did it begin?
And then I remember the years that have passed.
Living with Jesus they've gone by so fast.
I've staggered, I've stumbled. Not always walked
Straight.
And sometimes I've gone like a bull at a gate!
Yet Jesus has waited with patience and care
To pick me up, dust me down, urged me to dare
To walk once again in His footsteps, His way.
'But that means commitment,' I hear you all say,
'And loving and caring and listening too!'
Of course these are things that He wants me to do.
So do them I will in the best way I can.
Remembering with wonder just how it began.
I came to Him weeping. His arms He held wide
My need was so great that I hurried inside.
He calmed me, He loved me. What more could I ask?
And now in His presence I truly can bask.
Who cares about wrinkles? When all's said and done
I know that my Saviour will love every one!

B Bradley

REFLECTIONS

Alone I sit on this hillside
My thoughts passing to and fro.
The times we sat together
Now my heart is full of woe.

Listen, the chiming church bells
Echoing round and round.
Everyone is as different
As these flowers upon the ground.

Yet I see another mountain.
Away in a far off land.
There stand three awesome crosses.
Oh Lord, help me understand.

No sound of church bells ringing
Nor garlands of every hue.
For you a plaited crown of thorns.
Beatings they saw as your due.

The dark shadowy clouds of despair
Are chased by the light of your love.
Oh how I adore you Lord
As your peace you shed from above.

Your promises are always faithful.
Eternal yet ever sure.
Tranquillity now dwells in my heart,
Where once it was heavy and sore.

No longer alone on this hillside
Forlorn and full of care.
Thank you Lord for your goodness.
Sweet music now fills the air.

Daphne Wustrack

CHRIST'S MILLENNIUM

Christ will come again.
His second advent's near.
He comes on earth to reign.
Scripture makes it plain
His millennium, a thousand years.
Belief, hope and love, for all our cares.
It is there for all to read
God knows and blesses all who heed,
And reads, according to His word.

M Oliver

A POSITION OF TRUST

God created man and woman in His own image,
With a blink of His mighty eye,
He gave mankind a legacy, a position of trust,
Granted that day,
A position of trust, to serve God and mankind,
Beholding to no mortal, but the worship of our Lord.

One may look closely at what man and woman have done,
Many spectacular things, but dwarfed in a shadow,
A shadow of our Lord's greatness, the Creator, our God,
Who created man and woman,
And the many spectacular things,
Lest man and woman forget, the legacy,
A position of trust.

As we take a peek into the new millennium,
Many new things we will see,
Wrapped in science, medicines and machines,
Technological achievements, progress it may seem,
But what must not be forgotten,
To whom all this belongs, and who granted favour,
A legacy to all mankind, our Heavenly Father,
The Creator of man and woman who gave
Generations, a position of trust.

Brian Nichols

UNTITLED

Yours was the calming hand
That touched my worried face
Yours were the trusted feet
That led to this safe place.

Yours was the shining light
That took away the dark
Your vision was the ray of hope
That left its heavenly mark.

Yours was the voice inside
Telling me I could be free
Your heart was the strength
That opened my eyes to see.

You'd given me so much already
More than you really should
Yet still you took your place on the cross
And gave me your heavenly blood.

D Finkel

WORLD PEACE

O Father God you made the earth,
Created nature at its birth,
Designed all living things we see,
And gave mankind its liberty.
O Prince of Peace your will we'll do,
Your still small voice come shining through.

We look around the world you made,
The price of progress has been paid:
The calm serenity of life
Is often lost midst war and strife.
O Prince of Peace your will we'll do,
Your still small voice come shining through.

The blame lies with humanity:
Greed, hatred and insanity.
In Europe, Asia and beyond,
Lord be the world's eternal bond.
O Prince of Peace your will we'll do,
Your still small voice come shining through.

Retaliation, some would say,
Is quite the order of the day.
An eye for eye and tooth for tooth
Has been replaced by greater truth:
O Prince of Peace your will we'll do,
Your still small voice come shining through.

Upon the cross you gave your life,
So why should bloodshed still be rife?
Let's heed your actions and your ways -
Repeat *Shalom* and words of praise.
O Prince of Peace your will we'll do,
Your still small voice come shining through.

Michael G Salmon

THE WAY OF SALVATION

Two thousand years ago was born
A child in Bethlehem
Sent to earth by God, from Heaven
To bring a message to all men.

'You people I created
Have steeped yourselves in sin,
You cannot be my children
Until you repent and take my Son
To be your living Saviour,
And give your lives to Him.'

He died upon a cross for you
To pay the dreadful price
That I demand from all
Who are gripped in sin's cruel vice.

You must be pure to enter Heaven,
And Jesus is the key
To open the gate to Paradise
That you may be with me!

Audrey Coe

FORGET ME NOT

You were our life, our garden,
The beauty! That doth expound,
God's great gift bestowed on us,
Charisma to astound.

I know the willow, will always weep,
Yet! You are always there,
With mayflower, and daffodil,
Sweet scent, that fills the air.

Humming bees, and singing birds,
Over grass of emerald green,
That whispers words so lovingly,
We know! The Lord has been.

And under the willow, with guarded leaves,
In a special little plot,
Stands a blue, yellow eyed watchful flower,
That says! Forget me not.

W Lea

DISTANT DREAMS

Millennium, mile of difference!
The year 2000.
So near and yet so far,
My childhood like a star
Twinkling into eternity
Fading into nothingness.
Shell-like gauze of wings
Sorrowful memory brings.
Youth disappeared like sunset
Twilight years a dimming sight
From darkness into light
As the Bible said so bright.
Fragile gossamer thread
The children will need bread.
Innocence will never suffer,
Someone always will be the buffer
Churches open and churches shut.
Happiness, sadness, and fear strut.
Poverty or wealth is the state
Turning again the wheel of fate.
Bereavement raises its head
Always silent are the dead.
And long lost souls suspended
That history remembers ended.
Time is of the final essence,
Generations beget another -
Or a family tree decayed.
Trumpet at the last call sound
End of an era, an era begins
Millennium, mile of difference!

Valerie Kirwood Edwards

LOVE

Love comes in all guises
A pretty girl about four feet two
Hair so fair - eyes of blue
So clever with her fingers too
Little boy with his shirt tails showing
Mischief in his smile is growing
What he'll do next - wow - what's the knowing
A kiss that says goodnight, or morning
Or just - I love you - there doesn't have to be a reason!

Love shows in many ways
A card to greet you
A touch of the hand - as you walk down the street
So much more fun when two pairs of feet!
Love grows in many ways
By caring - and sharing
By saying - by praying for love.

Rita White

OUTSTRETCHED ARMS (MESSAGE FROM THE CROSS)

When I see you hurting
        so much that you
        don't know which way
        to turn;

I want you to see My arms
        reaching down, outstretched,
        to enfold and hold you
        in love.

I need you to understand
        that I came here for *you;*
        to be there for you in
        this moment.

I'm always here waiting
        for you to come to Me,
        and in the silence know
        I care.

When I see you hurting
        I want you to see My arms,
        I need you to understand
        I'm always here waiting.

Colin Gordon-Farleigh

UNTITLED

I will no longer wait, before the shield of hate,
Today, I put on the shield of love,
I throw away my angry sword,
I throw caution to the wind and
Put my reliance in the Lord,
Today, forgiveness offers what I need
To be free, who offers forgiveness for me
Forgiveness holds all I want,
Today I accept this is true,
Today I received the gifts of God,
Today by His will it's my will;
To willingly share in His gifts with you,
Peace I offer you; and all peace
Is mine to give as all peace is
Given to me, by the one who has
All peace to give,
Joy I offer you; and all joy is
Mine to give, the full goodness of
Joy, as all joy is given me,
By the one who has all joy to give,
And again I give thanks all the
While whilst I pray, for being a
Student of the word on the path
Of His most excellent way.

Alex Wallace

IF ONLY . . .

In glory it shone like a symbol that night
And lighted the traveller's way
That Bethlehem star guided kings from afar
To the manger where Jesus lay
I wonder if those, who had heard of His birth
Could have possibly known at the time
How that little child would follow the course
That His Father had planned for mankind
Jesus, by example, showed man how to live
By the rules, taught in His Christian home
And His Father in heaven, guided His Son
From the words, carved on the tablets of stone
These were known as commandments
A set of principles, for all nations to follow on Earth
But sadly, through time, man has made his own rules
And lost sight of their purpose and worth
Centuries have past and the world has advanced
An infinite knowledge we've gained
Through radical changes the planets survived
But steadfast, those principles remain
If only, all nations would follow this code
What a wonderful world it would be
Transgression would cease and there would be peace
A new-found joy in the world we would see.

M Lawson

COMMUNION

Altar bound
we go to
taste the
body and blood of Christ but I
fancy the blonde chorister sat
on the left. As I approach the
Sanctum she
winks at me
I wink back
and smile the
smile of one
who has a
guilty secret
in a holy place

James E Cragg

A PART OF GOD'S CREATION

I saw nature on a grand scale
The mountain heights, the valleys below,
The endless waterfalls and lakes,
The glaciers and the snow,

The frothing white water rushing over rocks
The crystal clarity of the mountain air,
The vivid greens of forest trees,
The peace and stillness there.

Some of the mountains plunge straight down
Into the fjord's waters cool and green,
And great waterfalls tumble in delicate cascades
Crystal clear and clean.

In the mirror still waters of the fjord
Are reflected mountains, clouds and sky,
Little farms perch precariously on the hillside
Way up, way up high.

The glacier arm stretches to the rocks
Towering over people walking near,
Ridged ice like polystyrene
Melts into the lakes, shedding its tears.

Yes, the very beauty of the landscape
Can bring tears to the eyes.
How wonderful is our creator God!
Over the universe His spirit soars and flies.

There is no end to His love, His saving power,
And we praise and thank Him, hour after hour.

Joan Marsh

A Gift To Share

I'm not very holy, not saintly and wise,
but I have a gift that shines from the eyes.
It speaks to the lonely, though no sound is heard,
and can lift up the low without saying a word.

No words are needed to give of this gift,
all it takes is a wish to cheer and up-lift
and a ray of God's love shines on its way,
just sent from the heart to brighten a day.

It shines far brighter, when to His words I'm true,
to 'Love one another as I have loved you.'
Then who am I to judge the path of my brother,
or cast the first stone at the failings of another.

If I were so perfect I wouldn't be here,
wouldn't have days when dark clouds draw near;
yet those are the times I can meet someone's gaze,
and be lifted by the light from their eyes ablaze.

For we all have His gift to shine from our eyes,
without being holy, or saintly and wise.
And if you can't name it, just think for a while,
Then turn to the mirror - and light up a *smile!*

Susan Carr

LORD I'M READY

Beyond the realm of life's prodigious span
I see a light, that beckons all is well.
Across the abyss, beams extend,
constellations, millions blend.
They blind me as I weave and wend.
From heavenly spirit they traverse far.

Another soul, another star,
my spirit, it hath shown the way
drawn me, close another day.
So much I earned, and now repose.
To wake, his wondrous ways do see.

'I'm home, oh Lord. Oh mercy me!'
His earthly plan for me is o'er.
Old Mother Earth my visit done.
'Did I score? Or has life just begun?'

To bridge the gap as we all must,
no pack, no staff, no material stuff.
The only need that we may have,
are stepping stones, hands known as dust.
The easier way, if the lights akin.
His wondrous beam will lead me in.

What is this torment I have within?
'Oh Lord please cleanse me. May I come in?'

Freda Ingham

You Must Trust In Jesus

In times of need it's easy to look this and that way
To a source of help and strength for something more
But it's where you look to that you'll receive from and be led by
Oh look to Jesus who said He would be with you and lead you right.

You could look to this or that one mere mortals on the way
But could they give the words that you need from day to day?
Or you could look up to Jesus who said ask and you'll receive
For it is only by His Spirit that your eyes will truly see.

And when Jesus seems so far away even clouds are too dark to see
And you feel so down and distant and not the strength nor will
to seek *Him.*
Turn to the words which God has given and in His name you
speak them
And the light of the God of glory will set you free.

No matter what thoughts come, no matter what you hear
No mater what you see, it's only truth that'll set you free.
No matter what you feel, no matter what seems real,
You must trust in Jesus.

Nick Stratford

OUR BELOVED EARTH

This jewel of the Universe so precious and rare,
Giving natural wonders for all to share.
She can give you everything you desire,
Look into her heart and truly admire.
This brilliant organism loving and true,
Needs action now for her rescue.
Tell her you love her, show her you care,
Ask for guidance with a prayer.
She's one in a million, our beloved Earth,
Let her know how much she's worth.

J K Raynor

REBIRTH

We cannot hear you; we cannot hear your word
What are we to do; what are we to say
Lifetimes come and go and still, you pause
As if in mid sentence across the ages.

You wait, you watch. The world becomes impatient
You ponder, you sigh. Allies fall away, oblivious to the spirit.
From generations down, beliefs diminish. Lord, help us.
A tornado sweeps through us, the world becomes cold.

A great deafness has befallen us - you speak but we hear no sound
Only our own transient mumble reaches muffled ear.
Some can lip read; and see great plans and the poetry of your voice.
That is the nearest we get. For still, we cannot hear; we cannot see.

And do not know if even you try to speak.
Our eyes, our ears and senses live in a blinkered, slow motion world
Perception too slight to witness your word, your gesture
You evade us, like a shooting star, unattainable.

Pray for us Lord. Pray, for we do not pray for ourselves.
We must start again. Lord, help us start again
Take us back, back into your heart, O God
And to a new beginning.

Martin Jackson

THE YEAR 2000

In the year of 2000
Is it the beginning or is it the end?
Of things to come or go

Shall we all know
In the year of 2000
We've still a long way to go
Will we all be baptised by then?

In the year of 2000
One day we will all know it will soon be here now
Where shall we go?

A new dimension
Never before reached
2000 years since Christ
What will be
Mind bending freshness
Unlimited awareness

Moving forward not back
In the year 2000
It won't be long now
Time and space
For this human race

Are we all ready
For what ever next
Are we all waiting
And relaxed
In the year of 2000

J Earl

ANTISEPTIC COMMUNION

Why do you not commune with me,
But live instead in Coronation Street,
Where you and you fellow watchers,
Several times each week, have replaced
The Sunday breakfast made of wafers?

You watch, absorbed, then speak
Amongst yourselves, not as critics
Saying 'that script was good', or
'That performance weak'.

But in a different kind -
'Did you see what Deirdre did yesterday?'
And, if not, then gleefully explaining
As though it were the news,
That you are sharing with your friend.

And not some work of fiction.
Thus your communion is with each other
And through a flickering screen,
But never with the Lord of earth and heaven.

Alex Calveley

THE FALL

It was Eve,
Not me;
Eve.

I swear I tried,
Said no -
Really.

She tempted me.
Offered me
Fruit.

It looked lovely;
She, too
Inviting.

But I said no,
Turned away
Sternly.

Come, she said,
Just taste;
See?

I couldn't refuse
My help meet,
Honestly.

So I bit
Forbidden fruit.
Luscious.

I knew then
Why God
Forbade.

One single taste.
Forever sent
From paradise.

Anne M Smithers

Two Thousand Years Of Jesus

The year 2000, what a date,
2000 years of Jesus, the world should celebrate:
Such a long time Lord, since you came to this earth,
And we still marvel, at the wonder of Your birth.

What Good News, 2000 years of the Lord Jesus,
The Baby in the Manger, the lovely meaning of Christmas:
You came to bring us your message of peace and love,
What has the world been doing, since you came among us?

The Millennium, 2000 years of the Lord Jesus,
And yet crimes and violence are still on the increase:
It is so very sad that not all the nations are now at peace,
And we long for the time when wars and hatred shall all cease.

2000 years of the Lord Jesus, how wonderful,
God's gift to mankind, You came to save us all:
Yet it is still not easy to convince some non-believers,
Of God's goodness, which extends to even the humblest.

2000 years of Jesus, is to Christians, something very special.
To remember the Lord of our lives, and to be joyful:
Thank you dear Jesus, for all you have done for the world,
Please watch over and help us, in the coming years.

Diana R Duff

THE FIVE SENSES

Life is a journey we begin by
Using all our senses
To bond close to our Mother's love
To touch her face with tiny hands
To hold her fingers to pull her hair
To see joy on her face

We listen to her voice, taste
The salt of her warm tears
And we learn to love and care

Touch is the most bonding
A baby may not be able
To see or hear, but learns
By the scent and touch of
Their mother to bond close to her

God gives each child a special gift
To stay with them to their journey's end
It will emerge at any time
It doesn't always show when young
It may be later in life

The gift may be only a special smile
Given freely to all
A beautiful voice, the gift of giving
Painting, musical, or
Even the gift of understanding

As we journey on our paths of life
Our senses play the greatest part
Without them we could not
Emerge into the person
God wants us to be.

Stella Hughes

LISTEN TO THE TREES

You can barely hear a whisper
Just a swishing of the leaves
A canopy of greenness
A cynic must believe
This peaceful haven calls you
If you're troubled here's your cloak
Of air surrounding sorrow
The breeze a gentle stroke

Your problems may be mountains
Your weary feet can tell
You seek an answer from the trees
They weave their magic spell
To calm and sensitise you
Each crisp leaf underfoot
Snaps out a tune to wake you
Your mind becomes astute

So let the peace enfold you
Escape the greyness, gloom
Drink heaven's soothing waters
Give yourself the room
To know the truth within you
And if wisdom can secure
The answers to your heartache
This oasis is your cure

Susan Mulhall

A Golden Memory

Memories are special, and you are one of mine.
My earliest is joined with one of yours.
On your very special day, it was bridesmaid I did play,
And this week I lead a loud applause.

For you have stayed together, through storms and windy weather,
In addition to the good and easy times.
So it is with love and pleasure, that I share your day and treasure,
The memories of years so fine.

Fifty golden years seems long to a couple just set out,
But in contrast to eternity it is small no doubt.
So continue on together knowing you are loved,
By family and friends as well as God above.

Yvonne O'Brien

SCARLET

They called my grandchild Scarlet.
I think they liked the name,
Like Scarlet, in Gone With The Wind,
I think, she'll be the same.
Her lovely bright angelic face,
The fibs she tells, without a trace.
She thinks it's fun to tell you lies,
You see the twinkle in her eyes.
Like Nan, there's a burglar in the yard,
He's coming after you, it's only Blackie,
Next-door's cat, coming to see, what we're all at.
She says, the hamsters, are out of the cage,
I'm sure she loves to see my rage.
I can't take all this, at my age,
But when it's time to go to bed you see
Her sleepy eyes, you see the smirk go from
her face, and then it's no surprise.
She'll grow up good and wonderful in time
And I'll be proud, she's one of mine,
Like most people, will say the same,
It doesn't matter, it's just a name.

Freda Bill

MERE MAN

Sometimes, I get it wrong,
I stumble and I fall,
I hear your voice guiding me,
But I disregard your call.

Sometimes, I think I know what's best,
And jump in without a thought,
No prayer or bible reference,
And then I come up short.

Sometimes, I have my ego,
It tells me that I'm right.
Surely if I go this way,
I'll be walking in the light.

Sometimes, I expect that God
Will catch on to my plan,
That the creator and eternal,
Will follow mere man.

Sometimes, I fail to realise
The errors I make each day,
If only I'd turn and listen Lord,
And see your perfect way.

For you Lord are the answer,
If I would only ask,
You'd pour out all your love,
And guide me through the task.

Oh help me to remember
That you answer when I pray,
That you are truly faithful
And by my side will stay.
Always.

Sean Nixon-Smith

WE BELIEVE

How shall they know if they have
Never heard about
The God of all creation
He made the sun, moon and stars
He formed a whole plantation.

There were many prophets in all
Who told of God's great power
There was Abraham who obeyed without question
Then God made him
Father of many a nation.

Then there was Moses of God he was
Called too
To lead the Israelite people from
Slavery to freedom, he knew.

For forty years they wandered
Through the Sinai Desert they trod
And God provided manna from heaven
For their journey ahead was long.

Now Isaiah saw this vision of the Lord
Seated enthroned on high
He argued and questioned
'Who will go for us?' alas there's no one else Lord
Here am I!

The disciples had already met with God
For three years of their lives, had lived
In the presence of Jesus, Son of the living God.
Jesus showed them His love and pardon of sin,
And of His Holy Spirit that he would leave,
So send the promised Holy Ghost for revival.
We believe!

J Hamilton

DAYDREAMS

I wandered down to the shore today
To see the waves dance and tumble with glee
So I took off my shoes and joined in with them
And I know they were happy for me.

I sat in a glade and gazed up at the trees
As they towered above over me
As a shaft of bright sunlight beamed down from above
It was the work of the Lord I could see.

I climbed to the top of the highest hill
With green fields and dale spread below
Cows gently grazing and stream flowing by
My heart was won over
How could I go?

I walked along a country lane
Strewn with flowers, brambles and moss
The air was clear, the birdsong sweet
As the rabbits scampered across.

I stood at the window at close of day
Stars were ashine in a moonlit sky
The birds were sleeping, the night was still
And I knew that God was nigh.

Margaret Turner

SCHOOL'S OUT

Summer holidays are here once more
        For six weeks, or maybe seven.
How will the time pass, each week?
        Will it be awful, or Heaven?

The children are out with their balls and their bikes
        In colours of every hue.
They are all very friendly, - at first,
        The holidays are quite new.

There's a ring on the bell, and a knock on the door,
        'Please can we have our ball?
It's in your garden, amongst your flowers,
        We thought we'd better call.'

To retrieve the ball is quite a task
        Searching amongst the flowers.
Hoping that none have been destroyed,
        And making it last, for hours!

'Where do all these kids come from?'
        We hear the neighbours say.
'They're certainly not from our street,
        Why don't they go home to play?'

There's a holiday club at a nearby church,
        But it's only for one week.
Quite an exodus at ten am -
        It keeps them off the streets.

Mums take it in turns, to take them all out
        To the sea, on the beach, in the park.
Laden down with food and drinks,
        And never return before dark.

The children have got some lovely tans.
       Their hair is bleached, and fair.
They still play together, in a quieter way
       And some go off in pairs.

Suddenly, there is a hush, in the street,
       The holiday is finally done.
All the children, in smart uniforms
       Go back to school, a new term has begun.

Joan Smith

UNVEILED

I was feeling down and weary, in fact I felt quite sick.
When I met a smiling young girl, with dark glasses - and white stick.
Thinking - 'Why should she be happy, when she can't even see?'
She must have sensed my query, for she spoke these words to me.

'I know the birds are in the trees, for I can hear them sing.
I can smell the rose in summer, and the flowers that bloom in spring.
I can hear the sound of music, and the little ones at play.
I enjoy the rippling of a stream, and the smell of new mown hay.

I can taste the good fruits of the earth, I can feel the sun and rain.
The breezes on the hillside, and good friends to meet again.
When they nailed my saviour to the cross, that day at Calvary,
I didn't have to see it, I *know* he died for me!'

With a cheery wave she left me, then I knew - as we did part,
It's not the vision in the eye, it's the one within the heart,
When I think that I've got troubles, whatever they may be,
I thank God for the angel, who taught me how to see!

Ray Smith

ONE PUTS THEIR TRUST IN GOD

One puts their trust in God
Who first puts trust in us
We live our lives down chosen paths,
Winding, turning, bending
Sometimes twisted ones.
God alone will help us choose,
The right one we should use.
There is no smooth and easy ride
Only the years of times we've tried.

Anne Freeman

PROMISE

Why do we cling to earthly joys
The taste of which is oh!
So quickly gone, and yet,
We blithely through the years
Take not thought for other joys
Which are eternal, yet to come.

If only we would take the grace,
A gift which is so freely given,
Then we with faith would truly see
This fleeting life, these moments,
Are but stepping stones
To Heaven.

Jeannine Anderson Hall

FATHER-SON

Toddler's anguished cry
Pierced garden serenity.
Secateurs dropped like hot coals
Father sped towards sound
Eyes scanning shrubbery veil.

Fear baited breath
Gripped chest tight.
Mind targeted prayer.

Relief's sigh lifted
Son's tearful face
From pierced flesh.
Young lip quivering
Son showed bloody hand

Giant splinter
Deeply embedded,
Wood nailing
Tender skin.
Stretching arms wide

Son gave himself up
To father's care
Trusting his healing powers,
Secure in love's embrace.

Julia Cutting

DO IT FOR ME

Be brave my little soldier,
The world is yours to see
You'll see it all when you are older,
Go see it all for me.

Go to places yet unfound,
By land and air and sea,
Experience each sight and sound,
Go do it all for me.

Kill monsters from the ocean deep,
Fight pirates on the sea,
Zap Martians while I soundly sleep,
Go get them all for me.

Taste spices from a far off shore,
Strange fishes from the sea,
Meats and fruits and so much more,
Go taste them all for me.

Go listen to the king of beasts,
And hunting chimpanzees,
Hyenas in a frenzied feast,
Go hear them all for me.

And when you're basking in your glories,
Come and sit upon my knee,
Tell me all your wondrous stories,
Come and tell them all to me.

John R Jones

MILLENNIUM DREAM

A new age has dawned for all mankind -
A time of progress for heart and mind.
A chance to put right the wrongs we have done;
And a better life for all to be won.

This is the time for peace to reign;
A time for our faith to rise again;
An opening for the words of love
That come with blessings from above.

This chance is ours - to mend our ways
And love our neighbours as God says;
To lend a hand to those in need,
With love and care in every deed.

Together we'll build a better place,
Joining God's people of every race,
With loving kindness, peace and prayer -
A future of hope and joy we'll share.

Bessie Martin

ABEL AND CAIN

Abel was slain by Lucifer the Devil,
We are the Cains, the root of all the evil.
We rape and rob and cheat
And slander one another
And happily repeat
What Cain did to his brother.
But Abel's pleas were heard
And plotted out the stain
The Godman came to Earth
And made us whole again.

Johanna Pihulak

THE EVIL THAT GROWS

How many times
when bad things happen
Do we blame
The 'Lord' our 'God'

It's not his fault
There's such evil
That's all around us every day
I say the 'Devil' is laughing
He seems to be getting
Everything his own way

This world is not very pretty
There seems so much bad around
It doesn't make the 'Lord' very happy
When will more good be found?

I shall keep on waiting
While I'm on this earth
To see this 'world' changing
It would bring us new birth

The Lord would be happy
The 'Devil' would laugh no more

I always leave my door open
For the 'Lord' to come on in
So he can free this world
Of such awful sin.

Trisha Moreton

THOUGHTS

Tempting at times
Frightening
Sad.
So many different thoughts.
A cream cake,
A noise behind a door,
A loved one, lost.
Shall I or shan't I?
Bite the cake.
Open the door.
Cry.
But wait,
My thoughts are all of me.
What of others?
They need me too.
They're sad and scared and tempted.
Where do they turn
To ask for help?
So many need our thoughts
More often than we do.
Let's pause a while
And think
Of them.

JML

WHEN YOU'D LIKE TO FORGET

Amnesia could be ignorant bliss,
But what of that first stolen kiss?
No memories to colour the mind,
Nor thoughts of people who were kind.
Why should we blot them from our souls;
Hide in holes like nocturnal moles?
In life's book we'd have nothing to write,
No catalogue about life's fight.
For surely, all we experience
And modern man's delirience,
Should be written for posterity.
Treated with integrity?
When we are octogenarians
Reflections are as precious gems
so, breath the purity of life . . .
Savour all, even strife.
Along life's road we're born to walk.
Recall all things: to people talk.
Communication's an opaque pearl,
Be he peasant, or be he an Earl.
From all encounters we recall
The versatility of it all,
Shakespeare said that 'Life's a stage,'
The clichê is fresh unto this age.
Be sure to drawn a firm conclusion,
Grasp all life with much profusion.
Where is the joy if we lose life's link
And suddenly don't want to think?
Hold onto all, then seek for more.
People make life, of that I'm sure.

Celia Ann Islam

STROLLING

A Couple strolled by the old Lych gate
'Let's stand awhile, and watch, and wait,
Said the lass with an envious look in her eye
To see the people all pass by,
Why do they come and go in there,
The lad replied, to say a prayer
And learn about God's love and ways.
Pooh, I learnt that in my school days
Remarked the lass with a scornful grin
I need no preaching from within.
Now, said the lad, I do not think it funny
I know God cannot give us any money
We have no work, no hope of fame
But to do God's will, must be our aim.
He gives us love, and warmth, and feeling
Which to us, is most appealing.
He like us - loves a loving heart
Which is sadly missed when we're apart.
He gives us all our different features
And instinct to all living creatures.
He tints the trees with a rustic hue
And nurtures them with his morning dew.
He spurs the seeds to sprout and grow
Into little plants that stand, row on row
As the earth and the soil responds to the weather
So God and man must work together.
Oh - I never thought like that, said the lass
I thought things grew like common grass,
Even common grass must have a thread
Of life, to raise it from the dead.
Well - they've a lively gait, and a spark in their eye
Shall we go in and give it a try,
We will not say the plea - I want
As used by children from the font.

We'll say, Dear Lord, we're tired of strolling
And smile and ask if He's enrolling
And if we ask both true and kind
A suitable path for us He'll find.

M Birtles

THE TREE THAT DIED OF SHAME (THE CHOSEN ONE)

Ashamed, a tree stood on a hill,
No other grew
It knew
upon the naked earth
its shadow threw a prophecy of death.

A single stem and twisted branch
Twelve leaves
One bright red flower
They knew
They too would die upon the fated hour.

No wind caressed the lonely tree
No bee prayed to the flower
No bird took rest upon its branch
They feared the tree's strange power.

Thus grew the alien
alone
each year one less
to wait the axe, the nails,
the crown of thorns
the infamy of fate.

Simon's hands, could ease the pain
Mary's tears could clean the stain
but no one
would recall
the name
of one lone tree
that died of shame.

G Jones

FREEDOM?

I'll tell you what annoys me,
Me and the toleration around me.
When I hear 'be free',
As if freedom is 'just to be'.

It's the society which can't see,
That rules don't destroy me,
That 'I' destroy me.
As if freedom is gaining every desire I see!

I'll tell you what breaks me,
It's selfishness which traps me.
It's the lie of 'self realisation' taught me
It's wanting to do things for me.

Who else, they say, knows me better?
Well do you?
It could only be the person who made me,
So maker have me.

It's then that love frees me,
That rules release me,
That serving teaches me.
And I am, well, truly me.

Andrew David Fisher

COWARD

Cool and green, inviting all,
The pool lies in the sun.
'Come in!' the friendly voices call.
'Come! Join in the fun!'

I long to be like them, so free
To plunge and swim and play,
But my own weak timidity
Keeps me away.

The tutor beckons: 'Come on in.'
I long, but am too scared.
The others gladly follow Him.
He called. They heard.

I'm safe, I feel, where now I stand
On old familiar ground.

But when the floods invade the land
I'm drowned.

Jean Healey

IMAGES OF GOD

God is a kindly old man,
His beard is long white and flowing
And I'm trying the best that I can
To meet Him and really start growing.

At least that's the image I have
And I would be quite taken aback
If the God of my mystical path
Was an attractive young woman and black.

T Woodhouse

MEMORIES

I'm looking in the mirror
I'm wondering who I am
Am I the girl who bore you
The girl who pushed your pram

The time has passed so quickly
The years have gone so fast
I find it hard to recognise
That I am old at last

I don't feel any different
I'm just the same inside
But looking in the mirror
I see youthfulness has died

I look at you in wonder
I stand here and recall
That you were once my little boy
Who played with bat and ball

And now you are a father
With children of you own
And I am just so proud to be
The mother you have known

Barbara Hampson

OBSERVATIONS

a single dust road
a cluster of houses blotchy from neglect
moss clinging to slanty roofs
sagging fences
unkempt yards
amidst a turbulence of colour
lavender, poppies, dandelions
bluebells and clover
feathery ferns
low, prickly bushes
gorse
nettles and thistles between ruts
midges feasting under clouds of dyed purple

a slate-roofed church, apologetic
an inn with a window open
on the sill bread dough
left to bloat under a tea towel
fresh coriander
a limp- daisy chain

the air shivers
a thin haze on the hills like a silken scarf
trees cast spindly trembling shadows
the wind, now keener
watches leaves flapping along the ground
until secret fragrances bring
fragile calm
to a lonely night

Alfa

UNITY

United we stand, divided we fall,
for unity is in the heart of the Lord
To love one another as Jesus said so
God's people united against the foe,
to conquer the enemy without and within
and see all chains that bind us broken
forgetting ourselves in every way,
let the light of Christ shine to his glory,
Sword in hand shield held high
onward and forward is our cry
In the strength of our Lord we will go
to fight a good fight,
a body united with the head who is Christ
drink deep from him the living well,
full and anointed to go forth and tell,
the good news of God's saving grace,
In unity, love and peace.

Margaret Dolman

UNTITLED

Let me shine for Jesus each day,
As I go along the Pilgrim Way.
Help me to show my love towards others,
Because in Christ they are my sisters and brothers.

Come to my Saviour come today,
Hear about Christ who said 'I am the way,'
But do not delay,
Come whilst you may.

Joseph McComas

DOES THE DOME HIDE OUR SINS?

The mob still spits abuse, defiles and draws blood,
Just as at Calvary, where Christ was nailed to the wood.
The same sort of mindless bigotry, this day still rules.
The same God created beings, we humans, blind fools.
From the land where Christ died, was it in vain, his pain?
To the Emerald Isle, where Patrick preached; on hill, and plain.

The hallowed earth, where the dead are laid to rest.
Becomes a battlefield, desecrated, no longer blessed!
Fellow beings, with blood drenched hands; kill each other.
A holocaust, what matter? A sister, son, a stranger or brother.
Was that sacrificial Friday, two millenniums past, of no avail?
Does man, not wish to rise! 'Neath the cross, despite the Roman nail.

These evil strains, which stalk the earth,
Reduce us all to what we are worth,
A speck of dust, little quality, at that.
Yet we dare, we do; to castigate, the rat.

Gerald M Fitzgerald

CHILD OF MY LOVE

Child of my love, come rest in me,
Your burden is great, as big as can be,
Weighing you down like a mighty stone,
Don't try to carry it all alone.
Child of my love, just ask of me,
Whatever you need I'll give you free,
I know of your pain, I see all your tears,
I know all your anguish and all of the fears,
Child of my love, give them to me,
Then your heart at peace will be.

C Brown

WHAT IS A PRAYER?

What is a prayer, I ask myself?
A moment or two to share
The feelings here within my heart,
In joy, or in despair.

When life is full of troubles
And no one seems to care
I put my hands together
And slowly say a prayer.

I ask you for your guidance,
For courage and for love,
To face up to my problems
With your help, from up above.

When there's great joy and laughter
I must confess I do
Sometimes forget to share it
In a prayer of thanks to you.

Sometimes when I feel guilty
Over some unpleasant deed,
I ask you to forgive me,
With sincerity I plead.

No matter what my prayer is,
I'll find your peace again
And to finish off my prayer to you
I simply say 'Amen'.

Karen Husband

LIFE

The sun will rise
The sun will set
The rain fall heavy or light
The moon will fill
The moon will wane
There will be day and night
The wind will blow
The snow drift down
And softly the earth will still
The spring return
The birds will nest
According to His Will
Trees will burst into life
Flowers will bloom
Light and dark the earth shall span
And man will make the same mistakes
He has since time began

Barbara Robson

CONFIDENCE

How can I say I'm lonely
When God is always near?
His presence is my comfort,
His love casts out my fear.

How can I feel abandoned
When God is by my side
Ready to help me on my way
With hand outstretched to guide?

Why do I fret and worry
About what may happen to me
When a loving Lord, has given His word,
That He always will be with me?

Kathleen Warneken

LIFE

What is life without
sorrow, struggle and pain,
work, concern and gain?

What is life without
truth, touch and love,
gently given from above?

What is life without
pain of a child's birth?
So it is on earth.

Marshal Green

MORNING LIGHT

Another beautiful day.
O God, please carry me.
The moments come and go
Slipping past so easily.

I ask your grace today.
Cover me from harm.
Vulnerable as I am,
Shield me from alarm.

Please give me strength,
Shelter and hold me close.
Please give me courage.
Give me love.

Pettr Manson-Herrod

WINGS OF PRAYER

The wings of prayer are limitless
No boundaries can them stop.
They swoop to darkest valleys
And soar to mountain's top.

They cover cares and worries
With a mantle soft and pure.
No matter what the problem
Prayer provides a cure.

Like a myriad coloured rainbow,
Or shimmering gossamer wings
Comfort for the spirit
The wings of prayer brings.

S Binks

RAIN

Raindrops plopped from glistening leaves
and slowly dripped from soaking eaves.
A lark exultant vent the humid air,
its liquid notes in happiness bare.
Round blackbird its feathers to preen
as the ground in hot sun lazed asteam.
Dry earth soaked up the fluid flow
each quivering root to gladly stow
the liquid force from clouds passed by,
sucked in eternal cycle from sea to sky.

S M Hall

A LOVE SO STRONG

I've come a long way
What's next I don't know
I know that you'll be there
Each day I feel myself grow
Each day I love you a little more
Sometimes I feel so full
Other days it's all uphill
Then you're there by my side
I've done wrong so many times
But you showed that I don't have to hide
No matter what you always love me
Even when I'm not all that I can be
When I turned away from you
Your love for me came shining through
You help me to overcome all fear
When I need you I know that you're here
You took all hate and guilt from my heart
No longer does it tear me apart
When I'm in your presence I know I belong
Never have I felt a love so strong

Amanda Steel

To A Country Lane

There's a lane I love to amble
With church that is triangle
Where they sing of God's creation
And give most willing donation
As you walk down small hill
There's a wondrous vision to fill
With trees flowers and bushes
Where soft breeze rushes
Where birds do sing
With joyful air of spring
Ho to take time to stare
And know that God doth care

R Large

SHOW ME YOUR WORD LORD

Show me your word Lord
and help me to look
to trust in your word Lord
and your Holy book.

Give me the words Lord
when I want to pray
help me to learn Lord
from your word each day

Teach me your words Lord
keep them fresh in my mind
and make me like Jesus
ever helpful and kind

Give me your words Lord
in my life today
Help me to understand
all that you say

Guide me and help me Lord
show me your way,
teach me to worship you,
teach me to pray,
to always give thanks
for my life
each day.

Helen Lockwood

BLOWN ROSES

Let us all give thanks to God,
For the parents that He chose,
Who, in our hearts, are ever carried,
As the fragrance of a rose.

They, who nurtured us in childhood,
Taught us how to love and care,
That our lives may sweetly blossom,
In God's garden everywhere.

They were Your caretakers, Lord,
And we, their children would express,
Your great love, through them expounded,
By their warmth and tenderness.

Further back than we remember,
To our needs they did attend,
Showed us how to grow in goodness,
By their love, that knew no end.

As their rose petals shrivelled,
And, in time's wind, were blown away,
So their lives on Earth have ended,
But their love, in us, will stay.

They, for You, built our foundation,
Made us what we have become,
That, as like them, we stand enraptured,
By the love of Your dear Son.

They would not, like You our Father,
Feed poison, when we asked for bread,
But with righteousness of spirit
Leading us, as You them led;

Oh what lessons their lives taught us,
We came first and they came last,
With Christ-like love they did surround us,
Holy love, always steadfast.

When, from heaven, they perceive us,
May they smile at what they see,
Find in our lives God has blessed them,
As God, through David, blessed Jessie.

May the life, which God breathed in us,
As He has done, each generation,
Be recorded to their credit,
In His book of meditation.

Lord, may we mature in spirit,
Join your wider family,
Bring to you, through Christ, our praises,
For the opportunity -

To, like our parents, work Your purpose,
Set our course by You, our guide,
Live to pay You every tribute
For You, Father, nothing have denied.

When we too become blown roses
May the fragrance we have borne
Of Your love, seed in our offspring,
That they are not by evil torn.

Lord God of each generation,
Generous, compassionate and true,
We thank You for our loving parents,
Who brought us, great God, unto You.

A A Allan

GOD'S ETERNAL PURPOSE

We view the universe with intense observation,
Beholding God's glory in His own creation,
Like prophets of old in their revelation,
For there, they beheld the power of God.
From the twinkling star to a green grass sod,
And the blazing sun at mid-day noon
To the sombre light of the midnight moon,
From the small insect, though wide the space,
To the intelligence of the human race,
All have a purpose within God's plan,
The chiefest of all of course, is man,
To him God gave the highest station
To guard with wisdom God's own creation,
The history of failure many do not believe
That Satan came Adam and Eve to deceive,
Yet, God's creation is marred all conceive
By human sin, violence and greed.
So, is this the end of God's creative glory?
No! Have you not heard salvation's story?
Far greater and glorious than creation's beauty,
Revealing the vastness of Christ's love and duty.
To Calvary He went with determined step,
No rebellion in heart, sin, or regret,
His Father's will He determined to do,
Providing salvation for me and you,
Fulfilling God's purpose for His original plan,
Preserving creation and His purpose for man,
Introducing God's kingdom with no regrets or fears,
That kingdom will last for milleniums of years.

F Sidaway

JESUS, MY BROTHER

Born in humility,
Part of a family,
Working creatively,
Jesus, my brother.

Blazing a trail for me
Through thickets called Calvary
Into eternity,
Jesus, my brother.

God's joy eternally
And very close to me,
Jesus, my brother,
Jesus, my Lord.

Kathleen Bishop

MISTRUST

Jesus loves me all children
that's what the good book said
So why do bad folk batter them
until they're almost dead?
How can an adult hurt a child
who cannot understand
Why they come up to smile at them
to take them by the hand
Then lead them to a lonely plight
while promising them such delight
Then their nasty deeds they do
and try then as they might
those tiny minds once filled with love
are damaged with such pain
So now they sit without God's love
and never trust again.

Marian Ball

INFORMATION

We hope you have enjoyed reading this book - and that you will continue to enjoy it in the coming years.

If you like reading and writing poetry drop us a line, or give us a call, and we'll send you a free information pack.

Write to :-
Triumph House Information
Remus House
Coltsfoot Drive
Woodston
Peterborough
PE2 9JX
(01733) 898102